Bus&Coach PRESERVATION

CW01021125

subscri...

Limited offer

Get 13 issues
for the price of 12

Plus a free copy of
**Leyland Buses
since 1955!**

LEYLAND BUSES
SINCE 1955
STEWART J. BROWN

telephone
01442 820580

e-mail **bcp@webscribe.co.uk**

Unit 8, The Old Silk Mill, Brook Street, Tring, Hertfordshire. HP23 5EF

SUBSCRIBE TODAY!

...ould like to take out a subscription to *Bus & Coach Preservation,* starting with the
_____ issue, and claim my special offer.

12 issues – UK £51.60 ☐ 12 issues – Europe £71.60 ☐ 12 issues – ROW £81.60

...Quarterly Direct Debit – £12.90 per quarter (UK – 12 issues only) **CODE: BCP175**

...ift Subscription Details (if required)

...Mrs/Miss/Ms: _____ Forename: _____

...rname: _____

...dress: _____

...st Code: _____ Country: _____

...No: _____

...mail: _____

...our Details

...Mrs/Miss/Ms: _____ Forename: _____

...rname: _____

...dress: _____

...st Code: _____ Country: _____

...No: _____

...mail: _____

...ebit / Credit Card

For credit/debit card orders, please call 01442 820580

...heque

...nclose a cheque to the value of £ _____

...ase make cheque payable to Presbus Publishing – Eurocheques are not accepted)

...er ends 10.10.14 – only open to new subscribers. Code: BCP175

...n time to time, Presbus Publishing may contact you with information or offers regarding subscriptions and other
...ducts. If you do not wish to receive such information or offers, then please tick the following box ☐

INSTRUCTION TO YOUR BANK OR
BUILDING SOCIETY TO PAY BY DIRECT DEBIT

DIRECT Debit

Please fill in the whole form using a ball point pen and send to:
Bus & Coach Preservation Subscriptions Department
Unit 8, The Old Silk Mill, Brook Street, Tring, Hertfordshire. HP23 5EF.
Tel: 01442 820580   Fax: 01442 827912   E-mail: bcp@webscribe.co.uk

Name and full postal address of your bank or building society

Service Users Number:

4	2	7	0	4	9

Name of Bank / Building Society: _____

Address of Bank / Building Society: _____

_____ Post Code: _____

Name of Account Holder: _____

Bank / Building Society Account Number

Branch Sort Code:

Reference (office use only)

Instruction to your Bank or Building Society

Please pay Presbus Publishing Direct Debits from the account detailed in this instruction subject to the safeguards assured by the Direct Debit Guarantee. I understand that this instruction may remain with Presbus Publishing and, if so, details will be passed electronically to my Bank/Building Society.

Signature:

Date:

Banks and building societies may not accept Direct Debit instructions for some types of account.

✂ ---------------------- ✂ ------------------------- ✂

The Direct Debit Guarantee (this should be detached and retained by the payer)

DIRECT Debit

■ This Guarantee is offered by all banks and building societies that accept instructions to pay Direct Debits.
■ If there are any changes to the amount, date or frequency of your Direct Debit (Webscribe Ltd) will notify you 10 working days in advance of your account being debited or as otherwise agreed. If you request (Webscribe Ltd) to collect a payment, confirmation of the amount and date will be given to you at the time of the request.
■ If an error is made in the payment of your Direct Debit, by (Webscribe Ltd) or your bank or building society, you are entitled to a full and immediate refund of the amount paid from your bank or building society.
■ If you receive a refund you are not entitled to, you must pay it back when (Webscribe Ltd) asks you to.
■ You can cancel a Direct Debit at any time by simply contacting your bank or building society. Written confirmation may be required. Please also notify us.

Introduction

This special publication celebrates the Leyland National, and in particular its part in the deregulation of the bus industry in the late 1980s and early 1990s. It is not intended to be a definitive history of the type, but more a colourful record of some of the many liveries worn by a bus, the majority of examples of which were delivered to their new owners in either poppy red or leaf green with no relief, the application of which was down to the operating companies should they be so inclined!

Leyland was keen to attract business outside of the National Bus Company, which it did both home and abroad, but the National will, in most places, always be remembered as the plain red or green bus you caught to work or to school.

One of the most innovative buses ever, the National featured a superbly strong and durable bodyshell which has also formed the basis of everything from DAB-built articulated airport buses to BR diesel railcars. Representing an important part of our social history over three decades, it more than deserves its place in preservation. It still looks and sounds like nothing else on the road, so, if you like buses, go and take a ride on one!

PHILIP LAMB
Editor

It's February 1981 and Ribble 459 (NTC 639M) goes about its everyday business heading for Wigan despite less than ideal weather conditions. PRESBUS ARCHIVE

A BUSES MAGAZINE SPECIAL PUBLICATION

Contents

www.keypublishing.com   www.busesmag.com

Editor: Philip Lamb

Design: Leo Gehlcken

Assistant Editor: Paul Cripps

Contributing Editor: Nick Larkin

Advertising: Sandra Lamb

Managing Director & Publisher: Adrian Cox

Commercial Director: Ann Saundry

Marketing Manager: Martin Steele

Printing: Precision Colour Printing Ltd

Distribution: Seymour Distribution Ltd

ISBN: 978-1-910415-08-5

Registered Office: Key Publishing Ltd, Units 1-4 Gwash Way Industrial Estate, Ryhall Road, Stamford, PE9 1XP

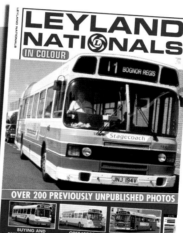

Cover: Seen in Littlehampton, Stagecoach Coastline 124 (JNJ 194V), a Leyland National 2 new to Southdown in 1980, awaits departure to Bognor Regis.

A National treasure

NICK LARKIN looks at the history of the Leyland National.

Never in the history of bus operation or preservation has a vehicle caused controversy, polarised opinions and even heightened emotions more than the Leyland National. National Bus Company subsidiaries forced to add vast numbers of the type to their fleets whether they wanted to or not, small post-deregulation companies which relied on Nationals to build their businesses, engineers desperately trying to cope with a vehicle undeniably more complex than its predecessors — all had something to say. The same was true of enthusiasts, who loathed the National on account of its highly standardised specification and the types it replaced, of passengers, sliding around on vinyl seats and longing for the comfortable moquette upholstery of vehicles that had gone before, and even of householders subjected to the loud wailings and smokescreens emitted. A lot has happened, and much has been said in the 44 years since the prototype Leyland National made its debut.

This was a bus resulting from careful planning, strong investment and indeed pride from its creators, who had come up with the strongest bus bodyshell ever built. But although the bus had undergone the most intensive testing ever carried out on a new bus design, not everything went right in the execution. As Mike Lloyd, who, as an engineer at London Country, the National's biggest operator, in the 1970s was responsible for helping keep a vast fleet of the breed on the road, says, 'I always had

the impression that they designed the bus and forgot it needed to be filled with mechanical units.' But people relying on the National for their living 30 years after the first examples were built had much for which to thank its designers.

National creation

Leyland had for decades been selling buses with its own chassis, bodywork and engines, and in the 1950s mooted the idea of an

integrally built bus built on car-type mass-production principles. The idea could not have been less popular had the manufacturer suggested that the new model be built from chocolate. The deeply conservative bus industry of the time wanted a bespoke product which allowed operators to stipulate their own specification and choice of bodywork.

The popularity of single-

deckers, which did not require a conductor, increased as the 1960s progressed, and in 1967 Leyland built a full-scale mock-up of Commutabus, sometimes known as the International, an ultra-low-floor integral single-decker with four axles and a roof-mounted ventilation system. Although the project was not universally praised, it provided the inspiration for Leyland to press ahead with a new design of single-decker

for the 1970s.

This was a time of great upheaval for the British bus industry, on both the manufacturing and the operating side. In 1968 Leyland Motors became part of the British Leyland Motor Corporation, and in the same year the National Bus Company was created by the amalgamation of the hitherto privately owned BET and already state-controlled THC

groups, commencing operations on 1 January 1969 with a fleet of some 23,000 vehicles. In 1969/70 the first Passenger Transport Executives replaced a multiplicity of municipal operators in four major provincial conurbations.

The bus industry in general was losing passengers fast and was desperate to cut costs. High capacity rear-engined single-deckers were seen as a way forward, even by trade unions, but with the exception of the Bristol RE,

the vehicles on the market were not proving too successful in service. Undaunted, Leyland's hierarchy persuaded the National Bus Company to set up a joint manufacturing venture, and the Leyland National Co Ltd was announced in July 1969. The then Labour Government supported the project, and a site was found in Workington, Cumbria (an

Seen here on demonstration in Eastbourne in September 1972 is FRM 499K, the last of the ten pre-production Nationals. Its livery, strictly not NBC, seems nevertheless a strange choice. Today, this bus survives awaiting restoration. PICTURES: PRESBUS ARCHIVE

Midland General XRB 419L was an early delivery, originally in blue livery, but by the time of this May 1975 view, had been painted poppy red.

area of high unemployment), for a state-of-the-art factory.

An extensive research programme began, involving experts from Leyland's car division, and the prototype Leyland National was unveiled at the 1970 Commercial Motor Show. Jaws dropped, although MCW's rival Metro-Scania single-decker took some of the limelight. A legendary quote came from the editor of Buses magazine John Parke, who asserted that the new product almost qualified for the adjective 'sensational'.

The crisp styling of the bus was the work of highly respected Italian car designer Giovanni Michelotti, best known for his commissions from Ferrari and Lancia, along with Triumph. The integral bodywork was designed to be repaired by relatively unskilled labour but was strong enough to withstand a roll-over accident. It was riveted together using an Advelok system in which the rivets had stems designed to break off when a certain clamping pressure was reached using a special tool. This was intended to make replacement of panels easier.

The extremely strong structure even had a successful performance in a car-industry-type crash test, the first ever undergone by a PSV. The bus would be available in two lengths — 10.3m and 11.3m.

Two aspects of the new National rejected basic principles and would hamper its reputation. Firstly, the heating system was located

Eastern National's Southend-allocated NEV 686M leaves the garage to take up service on local route 25. Later operators include Milton Keynes City Bus.

Another early delivery, Lincolnshire 2803 (UFE 805M) awaits departure. Note the lack of white waistband which was an optional extra — applied by the operator!

in a pod on the roof, with hot air being forced downwards, and secondly greyhounds do not run so well if turned on their side, which Leyland National clearly forgot with the 510 engine chosen for the bus. This controversial fixed-cylinder-head 8.3-litre turbocharged unit was launched in 1968 and met with some success in lorries but didn't really appreciate being turned over and having its various parts connected by an elaborate system of pipework. An additional problem was that the electrics were built in modules, which were fitted together, not always to the best effect.

On the credit side, a major effort had been made with ergonomics to create the best possible working environment. From the passengers' viewpoint the interior was undeniably utilitarian, with regulation vinyl seats, although the entrance was commendably wide. Much emphasis was placed on corrosion protection, with body components powder-coated and treated with an underseal that was also used on the

Queen Elizabeth 2.

The first National delivered to an operator, ERM 35K, one of 10 pre-production buses, was handed over on a somewhat ominous 13 March 1972, fittingly to local NBC subsidiary Cumberland Motor Services, with which it began

its career on Whitehaven town services. Of the pre-production batch a further two buses (KPA 101/2K) were delivered to London Country for its Stevenage Superbus operation, and a fourth

(MCN 151K) was allocated to Northern General, entering service with the latter's Sunderland District subsidiary. The rest were demonstrators, including the first left-hand drive example (DRM 590K), which was exhibited at the 1972

Amsterdam show. Delivery of production vehicles began with TXJ 507K, which entered service with SELNEC PTE in April 1972, to be followed by WFM 801K (initially registered UFM in

error), the first example for Crosville.

NBC had ordered 498 Nationals for delivery to its subsidiaries in 1972/3. Aside from five 10.3m buses (for Southern Vectis) all were 11.3m versions, in either dual- or single-door form.

However, although it was expected to take around 500 buses annually NBC was never intended to be the National's only customer; indeed Leyland had anticipated annual sales of

Poppy red and white Northern 4502 (OCN 748M) is seen en route to Coalburns.

Alder Valley 249 (LPF 607P) in dual-purpose red and white awaits departure for Guildford.

2,000 units, to a range of customers, including export sales, and although this target would never be achieved the National was far from being a sales disaster. That said, operators outside NBC were a little more cautious. SELNEC's first

Ayr, a member of the AA Motor Services co-operative became the first independent to take delivery of a National, XSD 789L.

Dual-purpose 'Suburban Coach' Nationals, with high-speed differential and high-backed seats, first

Green Line services.

Major non-NBC orders fulfilled during 1974/5 included 70 10.3m buses delivered to Greater Manchester (formerly SELNEC) PTE and 60 11.3m examples for West Midlands. New customers ranged from

In the early days the specifications offered by Leyland were highly standardised, this approach extending even to the livery, buses being delivered in a single base colour to which any relief (such as a waistband) had to be added by the operator. As the 1970s progressed, however, Leyland's desire to broaden the National's appeal produced an eye-opening selection of vehicles, including the flat-floor 'Suburban Express', the 'Business Commuter' mobile conference room and an extraordinary 'Lifeliner' ambulance version. A travelling bank was also constructed for the Midland Bank.

A superbly turned-out Crosville ENL949 (LMB 949P) demonstrates the leaf green version of NBC's dual-purpose livery.

batch comprised eight buses, delivered in the spring and summer of 1972. Plymouth was the first municipal customer, receiving its initial batch of 15 that same year, while in September Young of

entered service with Crosville in 1973 and were subsequently introduced by a number of other NBC subsidiaries, notably (and, uniquely, in 10.3m form) London Country, for use on

Taff-Ely to Isle of Man Road Services. NBC nevertheless remained the biggest customer, London Country alone boasting a fleet of more than 200 Nationals by early 1976.

A concerted sales campaign overseas resulted in orders from Jamaica Omnibus Services, which took a batch of 10 followed by 90, and from Australia, for which market an intermediate-length 10.9m version was produced, to meet local axle-loading limits; the National's construction meant it could be supplied in CKD (completely knocked-down) form. Closer to home, left-hand-drive 11.3m Nationals were supplied to the cities of Dijon and St Etienne in France, to Nederlandse Spoorwegen (Netherlands Railways) and to Norway, while a major cause for celebration in 1975 was an order for 450 from Caracas, Venezuela. However, resistance was encountered in various markets where operators remained keen to support local bodybuilders, and with this in mind Leyland developed a body-on-chassis version of the National, retaining the standard underframe and front and rear panels but with the remainder of the body built separately, the prototype being finished by Eastern Coach Works.

As early as 1974 Northern General, always one of NBC's more innovative subsidiaries, had extensively rebuilt one of its Nationals, moving the batteries and fitting new fuel tanks to improve weight distribution, and in April 1976 Leyland introduced a Phase II version of the National, which incorporated many of the alterations seen

London Country LPB 212P departs for Hertford on the 308.

first on the Northern bus. The batteries moved to a pull-out tray at the front of the bus, brake improvements were made, and buses came with revised handrails, along with strengthened interior bulkheads. For the first time moquette seats also became available on non-dual-purpose vehicles.

Having shown little early interest in the National, taking just six 10.3m dual-door examples in 1973, London Transport now took

delivery of a further 51, and, apparently satisfied with the type's performance in its arduous operating conditions, went on to build up a fleet of 437. Meanwhile United, which thus far had eschewed it altogether, took to the National in a big way, leaving City of Oxford as the only bus-operating NBC subsidiary never to operate the type. In 1977 the Scottish Bus Group, which hitherto had firmly resisted Nationals in favour of Leyland Leopards

and Seddons with Alexander bodywork, finally relented, placing an order for 10 buses for Eastern Scottish, which was suffering a dire vehicle shortage; further orders followed. In Northern Ireland, however, Ulsterbus and Citybus remained resolute in having nothing to do with the National, forcing Leyland to continue supplying the province with Bristol RELLs, for fear of losing its custom to Mercedes-Benz.

In 1978 came the option

Seen on service in Buxton is Trent 445 (PRR 445R).

Eastern National 1834 (VAR 894S) of Clacton garage picks its way through the narrow streets leading to St Osyth Beach.

of the B-series National, available only as a 10.3m single-door bus. A cheaper, simpler version intended to replace the Bristol LH in Leyland's range, it featured a traditional heating and ventilation system (obviating the need for a roof pod), a detuned engine and simplified trim; the principal customers were London Country (168) and Crosville (85). By this time, however, Leyland had decided upon more far-reaching changes

to what was now a generally respected product.

National 2

It was widely acknowledged that the National's greatest weakness lay in its controversial fixed-head 510 engine, and by the late 1970s Leyland was exploring the possibility of fitting the 680 unit familiar from the Leopard, using a Ribble bus, UHG 755R, to test the installation in service. At the 1978 Commercial Motor

Show Leyland exhibited a prototype National 2 (NCW 800T, also destined for Ribble) fitted with a 690 engine, this being a lightly turbocharged variant of the 680. Despite being an 11.3m bus it was finished to B-series specification, lacking a roof pod, but was otherwise visually similar to earlier Nationals.

Another prototype — a full-length, left-hand-drive, dual-door vehicle displaying registration CRM 928T

— was shown at the UITP conference in Helsinki in the spring of 1979, and the model was formally launched in November 1979 at the Scottish Motor Show at Glasgow's Kelvin Hall, where a short, right-hand-drive, single-door bus (later registered FAO 927V) was exhibited. These prototypes were instantly distinguishable from all previous Nationals, as they featured a more bulbous front end necessary to accommodate a front-mounted radiator, while frontal styling was revised to create a family resemblance to the Leyland Titan and the forthcoming Olympian. This added 30cm to the length of the bus but, together with the addition pipework required, was considered a small price to pay for the improved engine cooling and weight distribution conferred by relocating the radiator, which itself was cooled by a thermostatically controlled, hydraulically driven fan. The most important development, however, was the use of the well-proven Leyland 680

Making its way towards Redhill railway station is B-series Leyland National London Country SNB431 (YPL 431T).

engine — in this installation officially the L11 — in lieu of the 510, although in reality this was a stopgap measure (presumably to use up existing stocks) the intention being ultimately to fit the turbocharged TL11 unit that would shortly become familiar in the Leyland Tiger.

illuminate the entrance step and kerbside) and a lower step into the rear of the saloon.

Unsurprisingly, NBC was the principal customer for the National 2, the first two production examples being allocated to East Yorkshire, although the first delivered

new customers. London Transport ordered 69 dual-door 10.6m buses (for Red Arrow work) for delivery in 1981, by which time an order for 50 buses for Trinidad had been fulfilled. Despite being, in the main, full-length 11.6m vehicles many of the early deliveries for NBC and

as did the option of fully automatic transmission, and in reality operators could order a bus with a mixture of specifications — and in more than one colour!

In 1982 the turbocharged TL11 engine finally became available, as did the Hydracyclic transmission from the Leyland Titan and Olympian, but more significant to many operators (some of which had already embarked upon re-engining programmes of their own) was that Leyland now offered the option of Gardner's 6HLXB. At around this time the partnership between Leyland and NBC was dissolved, leaving Leyland in full control of manufacturing facilities.

A trio of Cumberland's B-series Nationals await their next duties in Workington in October 1984, they are from the left: 206 (AHH 206T), 214 (CHH 214T) and 212 (CHH 212T).

Other changes included a revised dashboard (from the Leyland Titan), uprated front and rear axles, while Leyland's publicity also boasted of a new, easier-to-maintain exhaust system, a front courtesy light (to

to an operator was FDV 829V, which entered service with Western National (in green but displaying Devon General fleetnames) in December 1979. SBG also took the type in respectable numbers, while several municipals became

SBG were completed to a simpler specification akin to that of the B series, with conventional heating and ventilation, and as such lacked the familiar roof pod. The full, A-series specification remained available, however,

The improvements introduced with the National 2 notwithstanding, demand for single-deckers diminished markedly in the early 1980s, largely as a result of NBC's Market Analysis Project, which envisaged an increased role for double-deckers, and the bottom effectively fell out of the market in 1983, in

Jones of Aberbeeg was one of just two NBC operators permitted to use a blue livery. Good colour views are rare, so please excuse this somewhat lacking shot of N2879 (BUH 297V) negotiating a tight turn.

which year NBC ordered just 52 Nationals, having now turned its attention to minibuses in lieu of full-size vehicles. Production of the National 2 finally ceased in 1985, by which time just 1,189 had been built, Lothian, Nottingham and Halton being among the last recipients. In all some 7,730 Nationals were built.

Deregulation

Although the Leyland National had ceased production a year or so previously the upheaval caused by the deregulation of Britain's bus-operating industry in October 1986 meant that the type now found itself in the limelight as never before. Faced with competition which threatened to erode their profit margins, incumbent operators were in no position to buy new buses but had vast fleets of Nationals which bodily were as sound as a new bus, even if the mechanicals were a little fragile. Many felt compelled to reduce their fleets in a bid to minimise costs, with the result that large numbers

Bristol Omnibus subsidiary Cheltenham District buses wore poppy red. National 2 CM 3505 (AAE 649V) is seen here in Cheltenham city on an 84 to Charlton Kings.

of surplus Nationals were released onto the market well before their time. Needless to say, the type represented an affordable tool to numerous new post-deregulation operators which were themselves in no position to buy new buses. Some shoved their Nationals into service without so much as a lick of paint, but others maintained their acquisitions carefully and even introduced their own modifications.

A number of the small post-deregulation operators, notably Chase Coaches, Yorkshire Terrier

and Birmingham Coach Company, became major forces on the back of their Nationals, which were often re-fitted with new Volvo or DAF engines and upgraded interiors. Major operators also bought secondhand Nationals, among them Lothian Region Transport, which despite having a small fleet of National 2s had eschewed the original model. Whilst disposing of its relatively youthful National 2s — themselves eagerly snapped up by other operators — Trent expanded its already large

fleet of Mk1s, and Go-Ahead Northern would continued to run its National 2s into the new Millennium.

On the following pages we bring you a selection of liveries from the post deregulation era, as well as a retrospective look at some of the Nationals to be delivered new in the UK outside of the NBC. It was never our intention to feature every one, we would need more than twice the number of pages for a start. Our apologies then for those omissions, we hope that they don't spoil your enjoyment too much!

Lacking any white relief, Ribble National 2 818 (YRN 818V) is seen loading for Manchester.

LT and beyond

Following comparison trials with the Metro-Scania, London Transport chose the Leyland National as its standard single-deck bus amassing a fleet of 506 including 29 National 2s They could be found almost anywhere in the London area at work on all kinds of duties including the Red Arrow. De-regulation saw former London Nationals sold to operators everywhere, many appearing elsewhere in this publication.

From the initial batch of six trial vehicles, LS2 (TGY 102M) is seen in Kingston in May 1982 having arrived on the 111. Later used at Gatwick and Dublin Airport, this bus is still extant at the Kells Transport Museum in the Republic of Ireland. PRESBUS ARCHIVE

LS111 dates from 1978. It is seen here when new at Golders Green.
PRESBUS ARCHIVE

New in March 1978 LS120 (THX 120S) is seen in October of the following year at work on the 248 in Romford en route to Upminster station. This bus later saw service with Bexleybus, a low-cost unit within Selkent. PRESBUS ARCHIVE

Seen here at Harlow railway station, LS30 (KJD 530P) wore this dedicated livery for the X99. This bus is today one of a pair with Overland Travel of Angmering, the last remaining Leyland Nationals in service. COLOUR ROAD

LS397 (BYW 397V) was new in 1980. At this time the 247 from Brentwood to Epping via Romford was London Transport's longest daytime service at around 24 miles. This National was one of a number to see later service with Parfitts of Rhymney Bridge. PRESBUS ARCHIVE

Westlink was formed by LRT in 1986 to operate tendered services in London's western and south-west suburbs. Privatised in a management buyout in January 1994, it was quickly sold to West Midlands Travel. The following year, WMT sold out to National Express, which soon sold Westlink on to London United. It continued to operate independently for a period, before being integrated into the London United business. Seen here bound for Hounslow in June 1997 is LS422 (BYW 422V). PHILIP LAMB

Capital Citybus was established in December 1990 as a result of the purchase by Hong Kong-based CNT Group of Ensignbus' tendered bus services in the London area. Following the purchase of Dagenham garage and 87 buses the operation was rebranded Capital Citybus. In December 1995, CNT Group sold Capital Citybus to a management buyout, the company passing to FirstGroup in July 1998. Seen here at Lakeside in May 1996 is National 2 No 741 (KRS 541V), new to Alexander (Northern) in April 1980 as its NPN7 and originally registered GSO 7V. Some two years after this scene was recorded, the vehicle was withdrawn and scrapped. PHILIP LAMB

Capital Citybus 749 (B359 LOY) was new with three doors to British Airways. It was to see later service with Imperial of Rainham. PRESBUS ARCHIVE

In 1986 West's Coaches of Woodford Green won the contract to run the 201 on behalf of Essex County Council. This service had replaced the withdrawn Epping–Ongar Tube shuttle, and saw the use of a number of Leyland Nationals including JTH 761P, which had been new to South Wales Transport in 1975. PRESBUS ARCHIVE

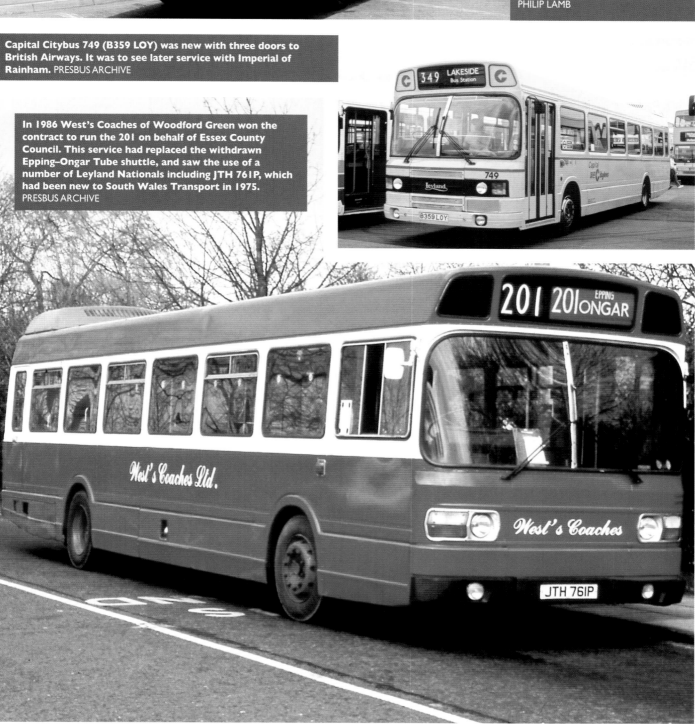

Around the PTEs

T he National was popular with some Passenger Transport Executives, with not all taking them in significant numbers. Tyne & Wear for example took just ten, whilst Greater Glasgow took 20. West Yorkshire had just 32, although NBC Nationals working in its area did carry Metro branding. Here we bring you a small selection, not comprehensive but we hope sufficient to convey the flavour.

Merseyside Transport Ltd was set up by Merseyside PTE as an arms-length company with a view to privatisation, which came about in 1993. MTL had several divisions including a Southport one. Seen here in Lord Street, Southport in October 1993 in No 6138 (WWM 916W). New in 1980, No 6138 was to remain at Southport for 19 years. PHILIP LAMB

South Yorkshire PTE bought 52 Nationals and National 2s including No 85 (JDT 435N) in 1975. The bus is pictured here in Huddersfield in August 1985. PRESBUS ARCHIVE

From 1986 until 1993, SYPTE buses were operated by an arms-length company, South Yorkshire Transport (SYT). At work in Doncaster in June 1988, SYT 1072 (FWA 472V), new in 1980, later found its way into the Isle Coaches of Owston ferry fleet. PRESBUS ARCHIVE

National Bus Company buses operating in the Tyne & Wear PTE area carried PTE livery but retained their own fleetnames as demonstrated here by United 3093 (JBR 693T) in Newcastle October 1982. This bus had been new in 1978. PRESBUS ARCHIVE

In July 1981 the West Yorkshire PTE and NBC formed the Metro-National Transport Company Ltd. PTE buses and NBC buses operating in the area appeared with a new emblem comprising the MetroBus WY and NBC 'double N', the two logos being linked to show that the two operations were integrated. MetroBus fleetnames were applied along with: 'The easy way from here to there in West Yorkshire'. Seen here displaying the branding is Yorkshire Woollen 156 (PWW 715R). New in 1976, this bus, following withdrawal was sold to Devaway Chester. PRESBUS ARCHIVE

Another Metro-branded bus, West Riding 133 (MUA 878P) is pictured in May 1985. PRESBUS ARCHIVE

West Midlands PTE took a total of 177 Nationals and National 2s. Amongst them was 1975 arrival No 4496 (TOE 496N) seen here at Birmingham International in October 1984. Re-registered MIL 7613 this bus was to see later service with McGills of Barrhead following the takeover of McGills by Arriva. PRESBUS ARCHIVE

Wearing a special livery and with coach-seating, West Midlands 6829 (OOX 829R) is seen in September 1979 at Birmingham International on special service 999. This bus was later sold to AA member Dodds of Troon.

New to the Council

Although the Leyland National was not aimed directly at the municipal sector, it nevertheless won the loyalty of major council-owned operations such as Nottingham and Plymouth, just two examples ot municipalities to build up significant fleets.

Barrow 16 (UEO 478T) was one 16 Nationals operated by Barrow, being new in 1978. It was later sold to McKindlass, returning home to the Barrow Transport Preservation Group with which it was finally broken for spares. PRESBUS ARCHIVE

Brighton took delivery of seven National 2s including No 29 (XFG 29Y), seen here in November 1988. Passing with the fleet to Brighton & Hove it was later sold to Bygone Tours/Nu-Venture of Maidstone. PRESBUS ARCHIVE

Burnley & Pendle operated many Nationals both new and secondhand. Seen here in September 1985, is its number 44 (XRN 44V), one of eight National 2s delivered in 1980. PRESBUS ARCHIVE

Chesterfield was another municipal to embrace the National operating both new and secondhand examples. Seen in July 1991, National 2 No 30 (OWB 30X) was new in 1981. PRESBUS ARCHIVE

Hartlepool purchased one of 14 Nationals new including National 2 No 14 (KAJ 214W) new in 1980 Seen in service in May 1989, No 14 was later sold to Stephensons of Rochford, Essex. PRESBUS ARCHIVE

Halton was another municipal to rely heavily on the Leyland National, buying many examples both new and secondhand including No 21 (ACW 21R). All of Halton's Nationals had a slot cut in the front bumper to facilitate towing. PRESBUS ARCHIVE

Seen at work in its home city of Nottingham in August 1997, National 2 No 710 (GTO 710V) was one of 40 Nationals purchased. This bus was to see later service with Barnsley & District. PHILIP LAMB

Seen here in September 1981 Plymouth 73 (WDR 873M) was from the first batch of Nationals delivered to the operator, the foundations of a fleet destined to total 57. No 73 was converted to a mobility bus whilst still with Plymouth, being sold on to see further service in that role with Kinch of Mountsorrel. PRESBUS ARCHIVE

Seen in June 1975, Lancaster 124 (PTC 124M) was one of three Nationals new to the operator in 1972. All three later passed to J. Fishwick & Sons. No 124 along wth the former 122 was sold to Yeowarts of Whitehaven in 1982. PRESBUS ARCHIVE

The Scottish National

Initial sales of the Leyland National in Scotland were poor, the Scottish Bus Group preferring the tried and tested Alexander-bodied Leyland Leopard, the mainstay of the SBG for many years. Small numbers of the National were though acquired, but it was not until the advent of the National 2. That the type gained anything like a foothold, even then only 123 entered the SBG fleets. Here we bring you a selection of Nationals new to the SBG and to Grampian and Lothian. Secondhand purchases are looked at on the following pages.

Grampian 72 (KSO 72P) was one of 20 Leyland Nationals delivered to the operator in 1976. Seen here in service, No 72 wad later converted into a sales and information bus.
THE OMNIBUS SOCIETY/ HARRY HAY

New to Eastern Scottish in 1977 as N763, National BSF 763S was transferred to Lowland soon after its formation. It is seen here in June 1991 in Hawick loading for Vertish Hill. PRESBUS ARCHIVE

New to Central Scottish in December 1978 as its N3 (EGB 80T), this bus, seen here in August 1986, passed to Western Scottish in 1989 becoming L580. In 1992 it was sold to A1 Service Member Hill of Stevenson remaining in that fleet until January 1995 when the operator sold out to Stagecoach. PRESBUS ARCHIVE

Again new to Central and passing to Western in 1989, KL770 (EGB 89T) is seen in June 1992 in Titchfield Street, Kilmarnock loading for Shortlees. PRESBUS ARCHIVE

On a wet day in Alloa in June 1991, Midland Bluebird 16 (DMS 16V) departs for Sauchie. This National 2 was one of 12 delivered to Alexander (Midland) in 1980. PRESBUS ARCHIVE

Also new to Alexander (Midland) as its MPN21 (DMS 21V), Fife Scottish 381 is seen here in June 1991 bound for Denhead. PRESBUS ARCHIVE

Completing a trio of National 2s new to Alexander (Midland) is Kelvin Central 1130 (DMS 27V) seen in service in Glasgow in May 1992. The following year would see this bus involved in a collision with a car resulting in a twisted underframe, leaving it beyond repair. PRESBUS ARCHIVE

New to Alexander (Northern) in April 1980, NPN7 (KRS 541V) was originally registered GSO 7V. It is seen here in June 1991 in Aberdeen awaiting departure to Lesmurdie and Thornhill. PRESBUS ARCHIVE

Seen in June 1992 in Kelvin's blue and yellow livery, KCB 1139 (MDS 863V) had been new to Central SMT as its N30 in April 1980. MDS 863V was one of several Scottish National 2s, having been taken into FirstGroup ownership, to be transferred to the South Coast to finish their lives with First Provincial. PRESBUS ARCHIVE

Threading its way through North Queensferry against the backdrop of the mighty Forth railway bridge in June 1991 is Fife Scottish 330 (YSX 930W). No 330 was to see further service with RoadCar in Lincolnshire — somewhat different terrain. PRESBUS ARCHIVE

Alexander (Fife) was an early Stagecoach acquisition, joining the fold in 1991. Here, in June 1992, 326 (YSX 926W) pauses in Dunfermline on its way to the bus station. PRESBUS ARCHIVE

Lothian only bought National 2s new, although a small fleet of secondhand National's was acquired to ease vehicle shortages due to increased demands as result of competition from First. Seen here in May 1998 National 2 144 (B144 KSF) later became well known operating a free service known as the 'Gallery Bus' between the Dean Gallery, Scottish National Portrait Gallery and the National Gallery. It was later sold to Horsburgh of Livingston with which it ended its days. PHILIP LAMB

BUSES

Buses is the world's biggest selling bus magazine, covering the bus and coach industry in the UK and beyond.

It is written and read with passion by people who care about the future of bus and coach travel, reaching an audience that extends from senior industry professionals to lifelong enthusiasts. It reports and analyses the latest developments — including company takeovers, new vehicle launches, route developments, infrastructure investments and key personnel changes as they occur, in an authoritative, readable and entertaining format.

Regular columns offer informed comment from experienced transport professionals, as well as a consumer's view of the standards of service that transport operators offer to the paying public.

Available every third Thursday of the month from WHSmith and other leading newsagents

 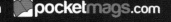
For our latest subscription deals visit www.busesmag.com

Kelvin Central 1124 (DPW 783T), seen here in May 1992, was new to Eastern Counties as LN783 in 1979. Upon the division of that operator, this National was one of a number to pass to Cambus before joining, again with others, Green's Coaches of Kirkintilloch, later passing, with its services, to Kelvin Central, whose fleetnames have here been applied to Green's attractive livery. Pictures: PRESBUS ARCHIVE

Gone North

Whilst the National, particularly in its original form, was not popular in Scotland, many secondhand examples crossed the border to either start new competitive operations or to bolster existing fleets following deregulation. Here are just a few . . .

Kelvin Central No 1108 (HPF 304N), new to London Country in 1975 as SNC 154 and latterly allocated to London Country North East, was acquired via John Morrow Coaches, the stage services of which were taken over in 1992. It is seen here in Glasgow in July 1993.

Also originating in Scotland with John Morrow, Kelvin Central 1106 (HCA 967N) was working the 5A to Glasgow Cross also in July 1993. HCA 967N had been new to Crosville as its ENL907 in 1974.

Another Kelvin Central National originating with Eastern Counties, No 1122 (CCL 779T) is seen heading out of Glasgow in May 1992 bound for Kilsyth.

Highland operator Alexander MacConnacher of Ballachulish dates back to 1919 adopting the fleetname Gaelic Coaches in the 1970s with stage services being added in 1986 under the Gaelicbus name using an eclectic mix of types including a few Nationals. Awaiting departure at Fort William in June 1990, HJA 129V was new to Greater Manchester PTE, and enjoyed a varied service life, being also employed by North Eastern, OK Motor Services and Pilkington of Accrington, with which it was converted to a Greenway and registered both PIB 7284 and PIB 5507.

Scottish Independents

Although the Leyland National had attracted little attention from the major operators in Scotland, independents such as Rennies of Dunfermline, Hutchison of Overton, AA, A1 Service and McGills of Barrhead all purchased the National new, albeit in penny numbers. Deregulation saw secondhand examples cross the border in this sector too.

AA Motor Services of Ayr operated a mixture of Nationals acquired both new and secondhand. Amongst the latter was SGR 106R, which had been new to United in 1976. The bus is seen here in Ayr in June 1991.
PICTURES: PRESBUS ARCHIVE

Starting out in 1978 with Crosville Motor Services, KMA 399T was one of four Gardner-engined Nationals sold initially to Blackpool Transport. Three of the batch were later moved on to Norfolk's of Neyland, the fourth (KMA 399T) passing to A1 Service member Docherty of Irvine. It is seen here in June 1991 heading for Stevenston.

McGill's of Barrhead built up a fleet of Nationals, both new and secondhand. Originally ordered by Crosville but diverted to South Yorkshire, AAK 112T was sold to Somerbus of Paulton in January 1989 moving quickly on in April that year to McGill's, where it underwent a complete rebuild, bringing the bus in line with its new owner's high standards. It is seen here some four years later, still a credit to the operator.

Clyde Coast operated a small fleet of secondhand Nationals including former Yorkshire Traction example N3 (WWA 122S) seen here in June 1992 bound for Saltcoats.

Amongst a number of new National 2s operating in the AA Buses fleet was USJ 491Y. New to AA member Young of Ayr, USJ 491Y is seen on service in its hometown in June 1989.

Nationals in South Wales

I n addition to deliveries to National Bus Company subsidiaries, the National attracted a good deal of interest from the numerous council-owned companies still in existence in South Wales at the time. Latterly good secondhand examples were snapped up by independents in the area hoping to make it into the big-time.

Captured here when new in April 1974, Pontypridd 14 (NTX 326L) was a single purchase, prefacing further deliveries to its post-1974 successor Taff Ely. This bus was ultimately sold to Rennies Dunfermline for spares. PRESBUS ARCHIVE

Taff Ely bought 17 more Nationals including three National 2s. Photographed at Glyntaff depot in 1974 is No 25 (RBO 35R). Taff Ely sold out to National Welsh in 1988. PRESBUS ARCHIVE

Seen in the bus station in its hometown is Merthyr Tydfil 192 (NHB 892M). Following withdrawal, this bus was sold to Redby of Hendon, near Sunderland, moving on to County, Leicester in 1988 before sale to Chase in the West Midlands in 1989. Merthyr purchased a total of 20 Nationals including seven National 2s, No 192 being one of the first pair in service in April 1974. PRESBUS ARCHIVE

Cynon Valley 18 (LDW 363P) was one of three Nationals dating from 1975 from a total 19 purchased. Local government reorganisation in 1974 had seen Aberdare, the municipal in the area, become Cynon Valley. Seen here in May 1976, No 18 passed to the newly reformed Red & White in 1992 upon its takeover of Cynon Valley, becoming Red & White 436, later Stagecoach 436.
I.T. LANGHORN/TRANSPORT PHOTO INTERCHANGE

Cardiff bought 21 Nationals including No 205 (GBO 140N) seen entering the bus station in August 1976. PRESBUS ARCHIVE

Red & White 447 (DDW 432V), seen here in February 1994, had been new to Cynon Valley in 1979 as its No 32. PRESBUS ARCHIVE

National Welsh/ Caerphilly Buslink N603 (SKG 913S) had been new to National Welsh as its 4077 in 1978. National Welsh was an early casualty of the deregulation era, being placed in receivership in early 1992. Shortly before that, however, a new identity for routes in the Caerphilly area, Caerphilly Buslink, had been introduced. Just before the collapse of National Welsh, this National passed to Red & White, newly reconstituted by Western Travel, upon its takeover of the eastern part of National Welsh. PRESBUS ARCHIVE

Glyn Williams of Blackwood ran quite a few secondhand Nationals including CBV 772S, originally Ribble 772 in 1978. Seen here at Blackwood in February 1994, this bus had, in the interim, passed to Southdown in 1977, being used in Portsmouth area, initially in poppy red with Southdown fleetnames! PRESBUS ARCHIVE

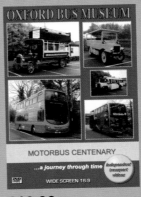

Seen in September 1988, Sheffield & District 104 (MHD 339L), new to Yorkshire Woollen in 1973, had been sent to wreak havoc in Sheffield by West Riding as a member of its Sheffield & District fleet.
PRESBUS ARCHIVE

Sheffield independents

Deregulation in Sheffield led to a number of operators cropping up all intent upon causing trouble for South Yorkshire Transport.

When SYT began operating in West Yorkshire as Compass Bus, West Riding set up Sheffield & District in a return move with services in the north of Sheffield. The war ended when both companies withdrew to their own territories, swapping the competing operations.

Elsewhere in Sheffield, a group of Preston Bus employees moved in a fleet of ageing Leyland Atlanteans. Operating as Sheffield Omnibus, commpetitive cross-city services were introduced.

Already a well-known local provider of PSV training, Andrews bought a number of withdrawn PTE buses, repainted them in blue and yellow and returned them to service, some on their old routes.

In another strand running alongside since 1988 was Yorkshire Terrier, whose fortunes are detailed separately on the following pages. We mention them here because Yorkshire Traction, seeking a foothold in Sheffield, bought out Yorkshire Terrier and its Kingsman subsidiary in 1995, a move followed by

its acquisition of Andrews, Sheffield Omnibus and the ingeniously named South Riding in 1996, these companies continuing to trade as Andrews Sheffield Omnibus.

In 1998 Andrews Sheffield Omnibus was merged with Yorkshire Terrier, continuing as a Yorkshire Traction subsidiary, but using the Yorkshire Terrier livery and fleetname!

In a further twist in the tale Sheffield United Tours (SUT) was relaunched from a garage in East Bank Road adjacent to that of SYT operating a network of competing stage services, the company staying

in business until the mid-1990s.

All this competition took its toll on SYT leading to significant staff redundancies, one group of former employees setting up in competition with SYT as Sheafline. SYT bought out Sheafline in 1994.

Old established operator Wigmore's of Dinnington, purchased by Duncan Roberts and Mick Strafford, was duly renamed Northern Bus. It built up a huge fleet including over 20 Bristol REs. It expanded throughout the 1990s also taking in Nationals, but was seen off by strong competition from SYT.

South Riding 8 (NTC 638M), new to Ribble in 1974 as its 458, also saw service with Northumbria.
PRESBUS ARCHIVE

Another former Ribble bus, South Riding 30 (PTF 729L), caught on camera in April 1996, had previously seen service with Pride of the Road, Hull. PRESBUS ARCHIVE

Displaying Andrews Sheffield Omnibus fleetnames, EFN 164L had been new to East Kent in 1973 as No 1164. This National, seen here in June 1995, was previously with South Riding and was the first vehicle repainted in the combined operator livery. PRESBUS ARCHIVE

Departing Meadowhall bus station in September 1997 is Andrews Sheffield Omnibus 2089 (SWX 536W), a National 2 new to West Yorkshire in 1981, and in service with both Keighley & District and Harrogate & Destrict before joining the Andrews Sheffield Omnibus fleet. PRESBUS ARCHIVE

Kingsman was a subsidiary of Yorkshire Terrier, born out of long-established Derbyshire operator Silver Service of Darley Dale. Here, Kingsman 62 (BCD 822L), formerly Southdown 22, departs Sheffield Interchange for Killamarsh. In the interim, this National had seen service with Topline and Portsmouth Transit. The livery is Topline's, later changed to that of Kingsman by overpainting the black with white — great days! PRESBUS ARCHIVE

New in 1978 to Yorkshire Woollen as its No 22, Sheafline 859 (TUG 806R) had previously seen service with Sheffield & District. PRESBUS ARCHIVE

Kingsman 61 (HPF 311N) originated with London Country as SNC161. PRESBUS ARCHIVE

Northern Bus 2881 (UTU 982R) was no stranger to the Sheffield scene having previously served with both SUT and Sheafline. It started out though with Crosville in 1977 as SNL783, which, given one of the Northern Bus proprietor's liking for all things Crosville, explains why it was still around and looking fighting fit in 1996. PHILIP LAMB

Yorkshire Terrier

Yorkshire Terrier was set up by three former South Yorkshire Transport (SYT) managers in 1988 to compete against their former employer on the streets of Sheffield using a fleet of ageing Leyland Nationals. The buses were garaged at the Keetona Works next door to the SYT depot on Greenland Road.

The company quickly expanded, acquiring a minority share in Sheffield-based operator Rotherham & District as well as the long-established Darley Dale operator Silver Service, which it renamed Kingsman, the fleet growing to over 50 vehicles, still mostly Nationals, and moving to the former SYT Central Works in Queens Road.

In 1993 the company bought five Dennis Darts, its only new vehicles, the National continuing to be the mainstay of the fleet, which otherwise comprised two minibuses, a handful of ex-British Airways Scanias plus the Kingsman coach fleet.

In 1995 the company was bought by Yorkshire Traction, which later acquired other local operators, namely Andrews, Sheffield Omnibus and South Riding. Consolidation followed with Andrews merging with South Riding and then Sheffield Omnibus whilst Kingsman was completely absorbed within Yorkshire Terrier. Yorkshire Terrier was effectively taken over by Andrews in 1998, although the combined fleet continued operating using the Yorkshire Terrier fleetname, the retirement of the many Nationals still in service following soon afterwards.

Yorkshire Terrier's green, yellow and white livery is demonstrated to good effect by No 5 (NPD 161L) seen here on the corner of Haymarket and Commercial Street in August 1990. NPD 161L was new to London Country as its LNC61 in 1972, later seeing service with Hastings & District. Travelling north to join Shearings emerging bus fleet, NPD 161L was acquired by Yorkshire Terrier soon after its formation. Sold on to AJC Coaches (Angloblue) of Leeds, it continued in service well into the 1990s.
Pictures: PRESBUS ARCHIVE

No 9 (GUG 123N) was a Yorkshire bus from the start, having been new to West Yorkshire in 1974. Following use by Yorkshire Terrier it moved over to fellow Yorkshire Traction subsidiary RoadCar, with no change of livery required! It is seen here, however, still with Yorkshire Terrier in Sheffield city centre in March 1989.

Seen in Sheffield's Pond Street bus station in September 1993 Yorkshire Terrier 23 (MBO 23P) had been new to Taff Ely in 1975 also as its No 23.

Formerly Southdown 86 (YCD 86T), Yorkshire Terrier 56, rebuilt to single-door by Southdown, reached Sheffield in 1991 via Thames Transit, most of Stagecoach's interests in the Portsmouth area having passed to Harry Blundred the previous year.

National 2s were not so numerous in the Terrier fleet. No 73 (UWY 64X), new to NBC's West Yorkshire, passed to Harrogate & District upon its formation in 1989 as a result of the break up of West Yorkshire into smaller units by new owner Alan Stephenson (AJS). It is seen here in Sheffield city centre in June 1997 bound for Darnall.

Yorkshire

The complicated sales and resales of NBC subsidiaries West Yorkshire and the West Riding Group resulted in an ever-changing picture enriched by the comings and goings of hopeful independents as well as the renaming of West Yorkshire PTE as Yorkshire Rider.

Yorkshire Traction 262 (TWE 262Y) was new to the Barnsley-based NBC subsidiary in 1982. It is seen here in 1989 in the operator's privatisation livery. PRESBUS ARCHIVE

Hull-based Metro CityBus started in a small way in the 1980s, the operator growing greatly when a large fleet of Leyland Nationals was introduced towards the end of the decade. Seen here in 1989 is its No 8905 (PTT 83R), which had been new to Western National as No 2843 in 1976, wearing both Cornwall Fairways and Cornwall Busways identities before arriving in Hull. Metro CityBus sold out to East Yorkshire in 1992. PRESBUS ARCHIVE

Part of AJS's West Riding Group, Yorkshire Buses served in the main the territory traditionally maintained by Yorkshire Woollen. No 143 (LRB 204W) had been new as Trent 204 in 1980. PRESBUS ARCHIVE

West Riding 184 (CWX 667T) had been new to NBC's West Riding as its No 49 in 1979, and was later renumbered 184. Privatised in 1987, under AJS it shared a corporate livery style with Yorkshire Buses. A huge fleet of Nationals was built up prior to sale to Caldaire Holdings, later British Bus and subsequently Arriva. PRESBUS ARCHIVE

New to South Yorkshire PTE, Compass Bus KWA 31W went North to compete against West Riding in its traditional heartland. Following the cessation of hostilities it returned to Sheffield, later seeing service with Sheffield Omnibus. PRESBUS ARCHIVE

LEYLAND NATIONALS

Keighley & District 285 (UWY 65X) is seen in August 1990. New to West Yorkshire as its 1523, it later served with both Keighley & District and Harrogate & District. Following a management buyout in August 1987, the constituent parts of what was West Yorkshire passed to the AJS Group in 1991, being sold on to Blazefield Holdings in 1993. No 285 had been new to West Yorkshire Road Car in July 1981 as its 1523. Following retirement at Keighley & District, this National 2 became No 295 in the Lincolnshire RoadCar fleet. PRESBUS ARCHIVE

A well-travelled National 2, Northern Rose 1515 (SWX 534W), new to West Yorkshire, was to see later service with Harrogate & District, Keighley & District and its subsidiary Northern Rose before joining Kelvin Central in Scotland. Like many First Group National 2s, it finished its days with Provincial on the South Coast. PRESBUS ARCHIVE

Rider York 335 (SWX 535W), seen here in March 1993, was also new to West Yorkshire, passing with a transfer of operating territory to Rider Group in 1989. PRESBUS ARCHIVE

Taylor of Morley operated several Leyland Nationals including AOL 16T, which had been new to West Midlands PTE in 1978 and seen here on service in May 1996. Before leaving West Midlands, this National was for a time part of the West Midlands Travel subsidiary Your Bus.
IAN LANGHORN/TRANSPORT PHOTO INTERCHANGE

Clarksons of Pontefract operated ABR 860S seen here in March 1994. This National was the former United 3048, new in 1977. PRESBUS ARCHIVE

Beyond LCBS

ondon Country Bus Services (LCBS) was divided into four geographical companies in September 1986, but today they are all practically totally reunited under the Arriva banner, taking different routes along the way.

London Country North West was sold in a management buyout in 1988 before being sold to neighbouring Luton & District in 1990, passing to British Bus in 1994.

London Country North East was sold to the Yorkshire-based AJS Group in April 1988. Following severe losses it was decided to split the company in two, forming two new operating companies — County Bus & Coach and Sovereign. Both continued under AJS control until 1990 when AJS was wound up, County Bus & Coach being sold to Lynton Travel. Subsequent owners included West Midlands Travel and Arriva.

Sovereign lost its Stevenage operations to Luton & District, but continued at Hatfield and St Albans, being sold to new owners Blazefield Holdings in 1990. Sovereign would be sold to Arriva in 2005.

London Country South East, renamed Kentish Bus, was sold to Proudmutual in 1988, passing to British Bus in 1994, whilst London Country South West, renamed London & Country and sold to the Drawlane Group in 1988, passed to British Bus in 1994 and with Luton & District and County Bus & Coach to the Cowie Group which later renamed itself Arriva.

London & Country SNB543 (EPD 543V), seen here in November 1996, was the last National delivered to NBC's London Country Bus Services. New in 1979 and now preserved, this bus was sold upon withdrawal by London & Country to Hall of Kennoway. PHILIP LAMB

At Redhill in January 1997 SNB394 (YPL 394T) wears a non-standard livery. Originally with Kentish Bus, at some point it had seen service with its sister company Northumbria. PHILIP LAMB

London Country North East (BPL 497T) passed to Sovereign following the restructuring of the company. PRESBUS ARCHIVE

Sovereign 699 (AYJ 99T), new to Southdown and briefly painted in traditional Southdown livery post-deregulation, is seen here in August 1995. This National, sold to McKindlass of Wishaw, finished its days in Scotland. PHILIP LAMB

Caught on camera in 1995, Kentish Bus 352 (SIB 1283) is a Greenway rebuilt from SNB479 (BPL 479T) in 1992. Transferred to Arriva Teeside in 1999, it was sold in 2000 to Blackburn Transport. PHILIP LAMB

Lincolnshire Road Car

The first Nationals to enter service with Lincolnshire were its Nos 2801-4 (UFE 803-6M) in April 1994. Seen here making its way out of Lincoln in January 1993 bound for North Hykeham is No 2801, which remained with the operator for its entire working life. This is the livery used initially post-privatisation, No 2801 being painted into later livery the following year. PRESBUS ARCHIVE

In 1988 National Bus Company subsidiary Lincolnshire Road Car was acquired by the Yorkshire Traction Group, itself privatised in a management buyout the previous year. Adopting a green, yellow and later white livery, Yorkshire Traction retained Lincolnshire Road Car's separate identity throughout its ownership of LRCC, which ended in December 2005 when the group sold out to Stagecoach, RoadCar now trading as Stagecoach in Lincolnshire.

RoadCar, as the company became known, left NBC control with a modest fleet of Nationals, their numbers being swelled in its years as part of the YT Group by acquisitions from both near and far.

Originally Yorkshire Traction 436, RoadCar 2842 (SWE 436S) demonstrates the later livery style. It's December 1990 and No 2842 is enterpisingly already advertising the 1991 Coachlink Holiday Brochures! PRESBUS ARCHIVE

2879 (DET 879V) is another former Yorkshire Traction vehicle. The National is seen here in August 1998 looking very tidy, belying its 18 years in service. IAN LANGHORN/TRANSPORT PHOTO EXCHANGE

One doubts whether the Volvo grille fitted to No 279 improved engine cooling any better than it did its looks . . . GTO 709V was a very early National 2, one of a batch of 12 delivered to Nottingham in 1980. Before leaving home, Nottingham 709 had carried a couple of all-over advertising liveries as well as that of Nottingham's South Notts subsidiary. In this picture dated July 1999, and with a fine view of Lincoln Cathedral in the background, No 279 is seen departing Lincoln bus station.
IAN LANGHORN/ TRANSPORT PHOTO EXCHANGE

Lincoln City Transport was added to the Yorkshire Traction portfolio in 1993, its operations being handed over to RoadCar, some of whose vehicles, such as No 296 (UWY 76X) seen here, could be seen sporting Lincoln City Transport fleetnames. No 296 was new to West Yorkshire in November 1981 as its 1534, subsequently becoming part of the Harrogate & District fleet with which it carried fleet number 290. RoadCar acquired UWY 76X, a National 2, seen here in June 1995, late the previous year. PRESBUS ARCHIVE

Starting out with Red & White in May 1977 as its ND1076, (NWO 455R) later became a member of the National Welsh fleet (an NBC creation which included amongst its constituents Red & White). Passing to Lincolnshire independent Barnard of Kirton Lindsey in 1992, it became RoadCar 2848 as a result of RoadCar's acquisition of Barnard's stage services a year or so later. PRESBUS ARCHIVE

United Counties 586 (SVV 586W) is seen in August 1990 in Bedford bus station wearing the short-lived United Counties privatisation era livery. Following service with United Counties, this vehicle was transferred to East Midland. CHRIS LODINGTON / PRESBUS ARCHIVE

United Counties and Luton & District

United Counties was territorially amongst the largest NBC subsidiaries. In January 1986, the southern area, that is Aylesbury, Luton, Hitchin etc, was partitioned to form Luton & District, the Milton Keynes area becoming Milton Keynes Citybus. The part of the company remaining continued to trade as United Counties and was sold to Stagecoach in late 1997. Luton & District went its own way, acquiring London Country North West and Sovereign's Stevenage depot, whilst Milton Keynes Citybus focussed on its city routes, supplemented by a small number if country services under the Road Car name. Today both Luton & District and Milton Keynes Citybus are under Arriva control, arriving by different routes.

Luton & District, initially owned in a management buyout, sold out to British Bus, and, renamed the Shires, passed to Cowie (later Arriva) along with the rest of British Bus in 1996. Milton Keynes Citybus was acquired by Cambus, which was sold to Stagecoach in 1996.

The Office of Fair Trading, however, required Stagecoach to sell both its Milton Keynes and Huntingdon operations to Julian Peddle in May 1997, who renamed them MK Metro and Premier Buses respectively. Premier Buses soon passed to Blazefield Holdings with MK Metro going to Arriva in February 2006. Here are some Nationals . . .

Luton & District 573 (MNH 573V) is pictured in September 1992 in Hitchin, This National had been new in 1979. PRESBUS ARCHIVE

Luton & District 423 (UPB 323S) has Stevenage bus station to itself — or so it seems! No 423 is newly repainted in Stevenage Bus colours following the transfer of Sovereign's operations based in the town to Luton & District. New in 1977 as London Country SNB323, this bus also saw service with London Country North East, Sovereign, Luton & District, MTL Manchester and finally Delta of Mansfield.

Luton & District 563 (KRP 563V) served in Aylesbury all its working life. Seen here in August 1995 in its hometown is No 563 in Bus Bond livery.

Arriva 3043 (GUW 475W), seen here in High Wycombe in The Shires livery, started out as a Red Arrow in London before taking up residence with The Shires in Luton. Later service would see this National 2 in South Wales with Parfitts of Rhymney Bridge and then in Hull with City Central.

Midland Red

A lthough Midland Red was very much committed to the BET-style-bodied Leyland Leopard for its single-deck requirements, and whilst continuing to take deliveries, did in 1972 start to receive Leyland Nationals in some numbers, and by 1979 around 420 were in service. Not surprisingly, with so many buses on the books, the arrival of the National 2 only managed to prompt an order for 25 buses.

In 1981, Midland Red was divided into five separate operating companies: Midland Red North, Midland Red South, Midland Red West, Midland Red East and Midland Red Express plus Midland Red Engineering.

One by one, these new companies were privatised. First to go was Midland Red West which had taken Midland Red Coaches, formerly Express, under its wing, in December 1986 in a management buyout. Subsequently becoming part of the Badgerline Group, MRW is today part of the First empire, Next to go in August 1987 was Midland Red East, by then renamed Midland Fox, also sold to its management. In 1989 it became part of the Drawlane Group, later named British Bus. Today it is in the hands of Arriva, as is Midland Red North, which was sold directly to Drawlane in January 1988. Midland Red South was sold in December 1988 to Western Travel, which in turn sold out to Stagecoach.

Whilst some of the National fleet was sold off at this time, many remained to become the property of the new operating companies.

In this crowded scene in Leicester we see Midland Red 822 (BVP 822V), one of the 25 National 2s taken into stock in 1980. This view demonstrates the last version of Midland Red's NBC livery — poppy red with a white roof band. The bus, having just entered service, awaits the fitting of a local blind. Renumbered 3822 by Midland Fox, this National was transferred by British Bus to Clydeside and re-registered VLT 204 in 1994. Following a short spell as a driver-trainer registered WDS 199V, it re-entered passenger service with McGill's of Barrhead in full livery upon the acquisition of that company by British Bus successor Arriva in 1997. PRESBUS ARCHIVE

Midland Red South simply added grey to the livery seen above to good effect. New in 1977 and seen here in 1994, No 627 (PUK 627R) later gained Stagecoach stripes. It was finally withdrawn in early 2003, by then 25 years old! PHILIP LAMB

Seen in Evesham, No 658 (SOA 658S) demonstrates the traditional-style livery adopted by Midland Red West. PRESBUS ARCHIVE

Midland Red North continued to use Market Analysis Project fleetnames such as 'Chaserider' as seen here displayed on its 901 (TOF 701S) caught on camera on its way to Tamworth in September 1989. No 901 later spent time with assosiated operator Stevensons before being transferred to Shrewsbury, where it was written off in an accident. PRESBUS ARCHIVE

Midland Fox lost its Nationals in the course of setting up the new companies, and so in time imported some replacements. Here, making its way through Loughborough without proper destination blind is No 2155 (GNV 656N) new to United Counties as its No 489 in 1974. The National had passed to Luton & District upon its formation and had been transferred by British Bus. PHILIP LAMB

Worcester bus station is the venue for this study of No 722 (WOC 722T) about to depart for Malvern Link. Note the addition of First fleetnames — no more West! PHILIP LAMB

MRN didn't seem to like being just a part of the old Midland Red as 'North' was omitted from its fleetnames, which latterly echoed those of the old company. The style is applied here to No 767 (BVP 767V) seen in Shrewsbury in July 1995. PHILIP LAMB

Stevensons, at the time Britain's largest independent operator, sold out to British Bus in 1994, its fleet and operations eventually becoming integrated with those of Midland Red North sharing a common livery but retaining Stevensons fleet names as witnessed here by National 2 837 (DOC 37V) which had been new to West Midlands PTE in 1980. Seen on service in Burton-on-Trent in August 1997 and later transferred to Shrewsbury, this bus is now in preservation in West Midlands Travel livery.
PHILIP LAMB

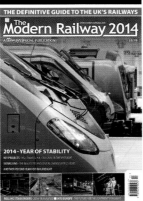

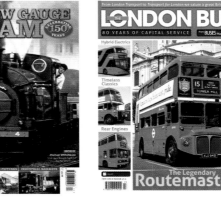

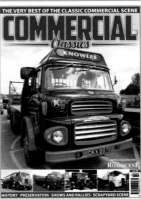

The Midlands

T he Midlands both East and West provided a great variety of operators new and established in the post-deregulation era. Here we bring you a representative selection.

East Midland, incorporating Mansfield & District, was sold to its management upon privatisation, the new company soon deciding to accept an offer from Stagecoach. Seen here in March 1989 in East Midlands' pleasing privatisation livery is its 515 (VKE 566S) which had been new to Maidstone & District as its 3566 in 1978. Passing from M&D to Hastings & District, this National also saw later service with Chesterfield Transport and McKindlass north of the border. Today it is preserved in Hastings & District colours. PRESBUS ARCHIVE

Long-established East Midlands independent Barton sold out to Trent's parent group Wellglade Holdings in 1989, but buses, albeit former sister company Trent's vehicles in the main, continued to fly the Barton flag. Here at Broadmarsh, Nottingham in August 1997, Barton 506 (ACH 506T) makes a hasty departure for Ruddington. No 596 went on to serve with Wellglade's low-cost unit Blue Apple with which it was written off in an accident. PHILIP LAMB

Here in Blue Apple livery is sister bus No 512 (ACH 512T). Like No 506, this National has been new to Trent in 1978. PHILIP LAMB

Chase Bus Services built up a large fleet of Leyland Nationals including several ex-London examples, YYE 274T, No 4 in the Chase fleet among them. This National was one of five acquired from Eastbourne buses, entering service initially in that operator's livery. Whilst at Eastbourne, it had been hired to Boroline and is still extant today in an all-over drab green livery. Chase was taken over by Arriva in April 2007. PHILIP LAMB

Long-established independent Stevensons was, as previously noted, taken over by British Bus in 1994, its fleet combining with that of Midland Red North. Prior to that however, we see in June 1990, National 2 No 135 (LUA 328V) in traditional Stevensons colours departing Uttoxeter for Rugeley. New to West Yorkshire PTE in 1980, this bus was sold to Somerbus of Paulton in 1992 spending just a year there, before joining Canavan's of Croy in Scotland in 1993. PRESBUS ARCHIVE

G. K. Kinch still operates today in the Loughborough area as part of the Wellglade Group. Amongst the buses helping it to achieve success in the early days of deregulation was HMA 565T, a B-series National which had been new to Crosville as its SNL565 in 1978. Seen here in February 1992, this bus was later sold to the Birmingham Coach Co for further service. PRESBUS ARCHIVE

The Birmingham Coach Co built up a large fleet of Nationals. Changing its name to Diamond, it became part of the Go-Ahead Group, under which it was merged with People's Express. Go-Ahead sold its West Midlands operations to Rotala in 2008. Seen here at Merry Hill in September 1996 is GRM 351L, new to Cumberland as its 351 in 1973. Under Stagecoach auspices it crossed the border to work in the Perth Panther fleet before venturing south to the West Midlands. PHILIP LAMB

Coventry operator deCourcey Travel today operates a mixed fleet in a white livery with blue and orange relief, the colours in different proportions seen in this June 1997 view of its National 2 GHB 223W, new to Merthyr Tydfil as its 223 in 1980. This bus saw interim service with Ogden's Travel of St. Helens. PHILIP LAMB

Metrowest 627 (NTC 627M) began life in 1974 as Ribble 447. Later years would see this National return North to see further service with Trimdon Motor Services. Former West Midlands PTE driver Keith Danks set up Metrowest to compete with West Midlands Travel on the 125 Wolverhampton–Dudley service, WMT eventually buying the company from him. PRESBUS ARCHIVE

Ludlows of Halesowen operated many Nationals in a white livery. Seen here in Bromsgrove bus station loading for Halesowen in May 1996 is TPD 194M, new to London Country as its SNC94 in 1974. Before coming to the West Midlands, this bus saw service with Southend Transport. PHILIP LAMB

B-series Leyland National Serverse Travel EPD 509V was one of many London Country examples sold on around deregulation. Serverse Travel started operations in early 1992, using two Leyland Nationals on service 96 to Chelmsley Wood, soon expanding onto other routes. EPD 509V is seen here in Sutton Coldfield town centre in June 1998. PHILIP LAMB

Bristol and West

In September 1983, Bristol Omnibus was split into two separate companies, the Cheltenham & Gloucester Omnibus Co taking charge of services in Cheltenham, Gloucester, Stroud and Swindon, whilst the remaining part was divided again under the Bristol Omnibus banner into two subsidiaries: Cityline to operate services within the city of Bristol itself, services elsewhere in Wiltshire and Somerset, including Bath, being looked after by Bristol Country Bus. In April 1985, Bristol Country Bus was rebranded Badgerline and in 1986 its assets were transferred to a separate legal entity prior to privatisation in September 1986 in a management buyout. Also that year, the Cheltenham & Gloucester Omnibus Company was sold to its management taking in Swindon & District. Renamed Western Travel, this company sold out to Stagecoach in 1993. Meanwhile the privatised Badgerline acquired the city services from Midland Red West, the entire operation now being in the hands of First.

Whilst still under the auspices of the National Bus Company, Cheltenham & Gloucester buses operating Gloucester routes were turned out in an attractive all-over blue. Departing Gloucester bus station for Painswick is GR 3076 (VEU 231T). PRESBUS ARCHIVE

Also in pre-privatisation days (1985), LH 1438 (GAE 300N) is seen in a special livery dedicated to routes 7 and 8 which linked Bristol Temple Meads railway station and Clifton. This bus was later sold to East Kent. PRESBUS ARCHIVE

On service in Bath in August 1987 and with no shortage of badgers on board, Badgerline BH 3079 (YFV 970V) makes its way out of the city towards Foxhills. In later years this bus would travel north to join the Northern Bus of Dinnington fleet. PRESBUS ARCHIVE

Same spot but eight years later and we see National 2 BH 3517 (AAE 661V) in dual-purpose Badgerline colours bound for Whiteway.
PRESBUS ARCHIVE

Bristol Omnibus took delivery of a total of 22 National 2s in 1980. Also from this batch, Cheltenham & District 3506 (AAE 650V) shows off Western Travel's livery to advantage despite the rain in January 1996. PHILIP LAMB

Stroud Valleys SD 3053 (SAE 756S), new in 1978, demonstrates an earlier version of the Cheltenham & District livery which used green and yellow for buses operating in the Stroud area. Later transferring to Cheltenham, 3053 would be repainted in the livery seen above. PRESBUS ARCHIVE

Nationals in the East

Eastern National took almost 200 Leyland Nationals, amongst them No 1899 (DAR 121T), seen here in Colchester in July 1995. No 1899 had been new in 1979. PRESBUS ARCHIVE

T he National was popular in both East Anglia and Lincolnshire. Here are just a few to see service in the east over the years.

Eastern National 1927 (MHJ 723V), new in 1980, was one of 15 National 2s delivered to the operator. Seen here in Colchester bus station in September 1990, this bus later saw service with Calderline and was intended to join the Provincial fleet, but was found to be defective upon arrival and so never entered service. PRESBUS ARCHIVE

New to London Country as its SNC95 in 1974, Southend 702 (TPD 195M) was one of a number of secondhand Nationals acquired by the operator. Seen here in June 1989, this bus subsequently found its way to the West Midlands, joining the Ludlows of Halesowen fleet. PRESBUS ARCHIVE

A former Nottingham National 2, GTO 704V is pictured here with Appleby's in Scarborough in June 1998. Before leaving Nottingham, this bus was allocated to the South Notts subsidiary and following Appleby's demise moved to Hull to enter service with local operator North Bank. It was subsequently to return to its roots when it entered service with Premiere of Nottingham. PRESBUS ARCHIVE

Kettlewells of Retford THX 196S was another former London example. One of three similar purchases in 1991, the former LS196, seen at Kettlewells premises later that year, was still in service with the operator in the new Millennium. PRESBUS ARCHIVE

Provincial

robably more than any other former NBC subsidiary, People's Provincial became synonymous with the Leyland National. The Gosport & Fareham Omnibus Co, fleetname Provincial, has a long and interesting history, here we fast forward to the early 1970s. Having sold out to the NBC soon after its formation, Provincial's operations were soon transferred to Hants & Dorset control, although Provincial fleetnames and leaf green, as distinct from the poppy red livery of the main fleet, were applied. Provincial was reformed as a separate entity in April 1973 by combining its routes with those of Hants & Dorset's Fareham garage, some vehicles also being transferred.

Deregulation saw a management buyout led by James Freeman, the name People's Provincial being adopted. Things moved rapidly with People's Provincial moving into Portsmouth challenging the ailing Portsmouth Citybus, and latterly Harry Blundred's minibus-based Red and Blue Admiral fleets, which sold out to First in 1995, Provincial following them soon afterwards.

Having introduced a new cream and green livery earlier that year, another livery change occurred soon afterwards when the green was exchanged for red.

People's Provincial fleetnames were initially applied to all-over leaf green buses. Seen here entering Gosport bus station in July 1987 is No 14 (HOR 414L). PRESBUS ARCHIVE

A new two-tone green and cream livery soon began to spread throughout the fleet. With the dual-doored former NBC buses continuing to operate in Gosport and Fareham, acquired single-door Nationals from many sources were latterly used to operate new routes in Portsmouth. These were numbered in the 3xx series as witnessed here by No 350 seen here in Unicorn Road, Portsmouth on its way to the then terminus of the 50, Clarence Pier. This bus was new to London Country as LNC28 for Green Line service in 1972. In service with Provincial in 1984, No 350 was sold on for further service with the Birmingham Coach Company, passing to Paleobus of Shoreham, where it ran for a while restored to original Green Line livery! Sadly, it has now been scrapped. PRESBUS ARCHIVE

Whilst the initial privatisation livery echoed those of times passed, a new brighter image was deemed appropriate, this appearing early in 1995, and displayed here, with First branding applied, in July 1996 by No 410 (THX 115S), one of a number of ex-London Nationals acquired. These dual-door vehicles were numbered 4xx and were used primarily on Portsmouth routes.
PHILIP LAMB

No 360 (RJT 147R) was one of a number of single-door buses transferred from Hants & Dorset upon the restructuring of 1983. It is seen here in Portsmouth in March 1997 in the cream and red livery. PHILIP LAMB

A substantial number of former Scottish Bus Group National 2s travelled south to join Provincial including YFS 306W, new to Eastern Scottish as its N306, passing via Central in 1985 to Kelvin the following year. It is seen here in Portsmouth in October 1996. PHILIP LAMB

Provincial's last National! Remaining in service following the demise of all others was National 2 No 432 (NLP 389V), spared because of its commemorative livery. New to British Airways at Heathrow Airport and with three doors, this bus was sold to Capital Citybus and converted to single door in November 1993, joining Yorkshire Rider in June 2000, before being whisked away to First Hampshire some five months later. Seen here approaching Fareham bus station, this bus was withdrawn in 2004 and is now preserved. PHILIP LAMB

Across the South

W

e take a trip along the South Coast from Weymouth to Brighton, occasionally venturing inland to view the variety of Nationals which could be found at work during the 1980s and 1990s.

A long-term Weymouth resident, Southern National 2823 (MOD 823P) is seen in the seaside resort and ferry port in September 1997. New to Western National, this bus was allocated to the newly reformed Southern National in 1983. This bus spent time in Sealink and Ferrybus liveries and towed a baggage trailer on ferryport duties. PRESBUS ARCHIVE

Hants & Dorset took 148 Nationals, amongst them 3744 (EEL 894V) in 1979. This bus was allocated to the newly reformed Wilts & Dorset in 1983, and is pictured arriving in Romsey in March 1997. PHILIP LAMB

Another former Hants & Dorset National, Solent Blue Line 423 (FPR 65V) was allocated to Hampshire Bus in the 1983 split. Taken over by Stagecoach, as No 3749, this National was sold off along with the Southampton area to Southern Vectis, which set up Solent Blue Line to operate them. Seen here in December 1994, this bus was later sold to Trent, passing in time to MASS Transit. PHILIP LAMB

Southdown built up a large fleet of Nationals, totalling 146. When Southdown was split in 1986, No 114 (ENJ 914V) remained with the 'new' Southdown and is pictured here recently repainted in traditional Southdown livery, at the time making a welcome return. Passing to Stagecoach with the operator, No 114 received Stagecoach stripes before being sold to the Abundant Life Centre of Bradford. PRESBUS ARCHIVE

Haven Coaches of Newhaven operated between Brighton and Seaford using a mix of vehicles. The operation was taken over by Blue Triangle of Rainham, the new incumbent drafting in some of its own buses including former London National AYR 300T previously used in London with Blue Triangle. The bus is seen in Brighton in August 1995. PRESBUS ARCHIVE

New in 1977, Maidstone & District 2904 (SKN 904R) is seen here in Maidstone in Park & Ride livery in June 1994 when 17 years old — it wasn't the newest buses on such duties back then! This bus would later pass to Fuggles of Benenden. PRESBUS ARCHIVE

Privatised municipal Boroline, Maidstone won a number of tendered London services including the 492, on which we see its 902 (AYR 345T), formerly London LS345. PRESBUS ARCHIVE

Split from Southdown in 1986, Brighton & Hove was allocated a number of Leyland Nationals and National 2s. Further secondhand acquisitions included former Yorkshire Traction 403 FHE 403L, new to that operator in 1973. PRESBUS ARCHIVE

The North East

NBC's subsidiaries in the North East, Northern and United both played a significant role as privatised companies. In particular, Northern formed the basis of what is now

the Go-Ahead Group with subsidiaries across the South and in the East as well as in its North East homeland. United turned out to be Humpty Dumpty in reverse, with Arriva actually succeeding in

putting it all together again. In the meantime, some of the most striking liveries of the deregulation era, such as Northumbria and Tees & District remain memorable almost 20 years on.

Seen in July 1990, Go-Ahead Northern 4609 (XBR 609R), originally ordered by Ribble, had been new to Northern General in 1977. Go-Ahead Northern was formed as a result of a management buyout in 1987.
PRESBUS ARCHIVE

Wear Buses was a Go-Ahead Northern subsidiary operating in the Sunderland area. No 4688 (BGR 688W), seen here in February 1994, had been new to Northern General in 1980.
PRESBUS ARCHIVE

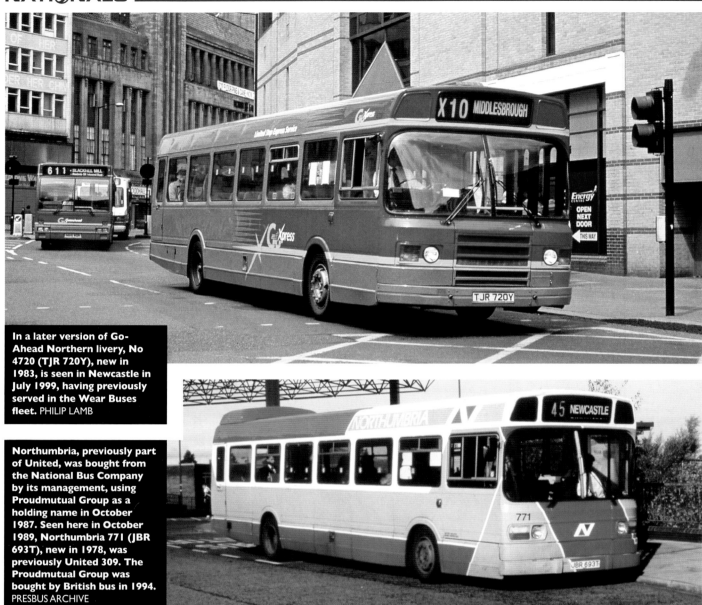

In a later version of Go-Ahead Northern livery, No 4720 (TJR 720Y), new in 1983, is seen in Newcastle in July 1999, having previously served in the Wear Buses fleet. PHILIP LAMB

Northumbria, previously part of United, was bought from the National Bus Company by its management, using Proudmutual Group as a holding name in October 1987. Seen here in October 1989, Northumbria 771 (JBR 693T), new in 1978, was previously United 309. The Proudmutual Group was bought by British bus in 1994. PRESBUS ARCHIVE

In 1987, the remainder of United, but not including its Cleveland and Middlesbrough operations, still trading as United. was sold to Caldaire Holdings which had purchased the West Riding Group. New in 1983 as Ribble 898 (ARN 898Y) United 3150 was caught on camera in Durham in June 1999, in the interim, this National 2 having seen service with both Cumberland and Shearings. In 1995, United was sold to the Westcourt Group before being sold on again to West Midlands Travel and then in 1996 to British Bus which in turn was sold to the Cowie Group. PRESBUS ARCHIVE

United's Cleveland and Middlesbrough operations were separated and renamed Tees & District, with the Stockton-on-Tees depot operating as Teesside Motor Services (TMS) under the auspices of Caldaire. Seen here in Hartlepool in March 1990 is Gardner-engined National 2 Tees 3140 (A140 FDC), new as United 3140 in 1984. PRESBUS ARCHIVE

TMS 3663 (ROK 471M) is seen at work in March 1997. This National was new in 1974 to West Midlands PTE as its 4471. It was later allocated to WMPTE subsidiary Metrowest. PRESBUS ARCHIVE

Stagecoach stripes

As the 1990s progressed, and the 'big three' operating companies developed, corporate liveries followed closely behind. It was, however, really only Stagecoach which, having introduced a corporate image ahead of its rivals, operated the National displaying its nationwide image in any significant numbers. Here then is a selection of striped Nationals, and as can be seen, not all were red, orange and blue . . .

Seen awaiting their next duties at Northampton's Greyfriars bus station in May 1991 are United Counties 546/61 (BVV 546T, KRP 561V), which had been new in 1979/80. United Counties was split into three operating companies in the run up to privatisation: Luton & District in the South, Milton Keynes Citybus with a new 'slimmer' United Counties continuing in the remaining part of the company's traditional operating territory. The new United Counties joined the Stagecoach empire in November 1987, the corporate image being quickly applied. These were the early days of Stagecoach when local fleetnames etc were retained, but, as can be seen, were not always applied in a uniform way!
PRESBUS ARCHIVE/CHRIS LODINGTON

The National's lines were well suited to Stagecoach stripes, subsidiaries in the south taking it upon themselves to add further stripes at the front of vehicles, an unauthorised practice that was ultimately discontinued. The extra stripes were, however, still in evidence in this May 1997 view of South Coast Buses 169 (WYJ 169S) leaving Eastbourne for Hastings. No 169 had been new to Southdown in 1978.
PHILIP LAMB

Bristol Omnibus acquired a large fleet of Nationals and National 2s prior to being broken up into a number smaller units in the run-up to privatisation. Amongst them was No 371 (AAE 665V), which latterly found its way into the Swindon & District fleet. In 1986 control of Swindon & District passed to Cheltenham & Gloucester resulting in a new company, Western Travel being incorporated to take over the combined operation. Western Travel was promptly privatised in a management buy-out, expanding further the following year by acquiring Midland Red South. In 1993 Circle Line of Gloucester joined the fold, the entire operation being sold to Stagecoach by the end of the year. No 371 is seen in Swindon in March 1997.
PHILIP LAMB

There were few variations to the Stagecoach livery, one notable one being the application of three red stripes to vehicles operating in the Sussex Bus fleet. Sussex Bus, based in Chichester and taken over in 1996, was to keep its individual identity into the new Millennium. Amongst those to wear the Sussex Bus livery variation was a pair of Leyland National 2s, of which No 128 (FDV 831V) is seen here at rest in Chichester bus station in June 2000. No 128, new to Devon General as its 831 in 1981, passed to Stagecoach in 1989. PHILIP LAMB

Seen freshly painted in Blackburn in December 1996, Stagecoach Ribble 904 (CWX 669T) is an early Greenway conversion. CWX 669T started life as West Riding 51 in 1979; later passing to SUT, with which operator it was rebuilt to Greenway specification in 1992. Operating for a time in Sheaf Line colours, CWX 669T was later absorbed into the Mainline fleet receiving fleet number 806. Next stop was Hyndburn Transport in which fleet it was numbered 59. Hyndburn was taken over by Stagecoach in 1996, the operation soon being merged into sister company Ribble. PHILIP LAMB

The North West

De-regulation encouraged many small operators in the North West, and in particular in Manchester and Liverpool, to expand, or to start from scratch, many using Leyland Nationals. Here we bring you a selection from fleets both major and minor.

Displaying to advantage Ribble's privatisation livery is its 888 (ARN 888Y), new in 1983 and pictured here in May 1989. It was later converted into to a café. PRESBUS ARCHIVE

Using the name Bee Line Buzz Co, United Transport started a minibus operation in Manchester in 1987. This was sold to Stagecoach the following year, but was quickly sold on again to Drawlane (later British Bus), with which it became a subsidiary of its North Western and began to operate full-sized buses. North Western had been reformed to take over the southern extent of Ribble's operating territory by NBC and by the time in question had become part of the Drawlane Group. Bee Line vehicles were latterly branded North Western Bee Line as demonstrated here by Leyland National 405 (MIL 5575) in service in Manchester. PHILIP LAMB

Without its Welsh operations, the post-deregulation version of Crosville soon broke up. However, prior to that a Brunswick green and cream livery with leaping Lynx logos was established. It is seen here modelled by SNL807 (WFM 807L), which had been new to Crosville in 1972. PRESBUS ARCHIVE

Cumberland Motor Services took over Ribble's northern territory in 1986, and was sold to Stagecoach in 1989, the status quo being effectively restored! In the meantime Cumberland Motor Services had established a pleasing identity as displayed here in July 1990 by No 366 (GAO 708N). New in 1974, it later crossed the border to join the fleet of McKindless of Wishaw, passing with its service work to Kelvin Central when it purchased that side of the business. PRESBUS ARCHIVE

Isle of Man National Transport 29 (MAN 29N) was one of several Nationals to operate on the Isle of Man. Seen here in fleet livery; this bus received a Douglas Corporation Heritage livery in 1993. PRESBUS ARCHIVE

LEYLAND NATIONALS

John Fishwick & Sons of Leyland operated many former Leyland demonstrators such as its No 15 (NRN 838P). PRESBUS ARCHIVE

CMT Buses established a major route system in Liverpool operated by a large fleet of Leyland Nationals including No 1073 (SPC 284R), which had been new to London Country, later London Country North East, in 1977 as SNB284. The operation having been sold to GTL, the CMT identity eventually disappeared. PHILIP LAMB

Liverline was another Liverpool independent, in this instance taken into Drawlane ownership becoming a North Western subsidiary. Seen here in Whitechapel in April 1994 is its 317 (YFY 7M), new to Southport and passing to Merseyside PTE. It had been sold to Preston prior to joining Liverline. PRESBUS ARCHIVE

Coach operator Shearings was quick to exploit the new opportunities offered by deregulation starting competitive services in several areas including Liverpool straight away. Pictured here in that city in September 1987 is No 48 (HHA 148L) purchased from West Midlands PTE in 1986, but originally Midland Red 148 in 1973, passing to WMPTE with Midland Red's West Midlands services. PRESBUS ARCHIVE

One of a large fleet of secondhand Nationals, Pennine of Gargrave's LN1 (JIL 2794), seen in July 1995, was new to London Country as SNB282 (SPC 282R), passing to Kentish Bus upon the split of London Country and subsequently transferred to Northumbria. PRESBUS ARCHIVE

Later developments

NICK LARKIN examines some of the measures taken to keep the National relevant to an ever-changing market.

Among the larger groups that emerged as the operating market began to settle down in the early 1990s was Drawlane, which acquired (amongst other operations) significant parts of what had once been Midland Red and London Country and as such inherited a large number of Leyland Nationals. Although the mechanicals and exterior panels were by now showing their age, close examination of a London & Country example revealed a remarkably sound structure. Thus was born what became known as the Greenway project (the name deriving from a re-branding of part of L&C's operations), whereby tired Nationals were 'remanufactured' for further service. Although intended as in-house exercise, it was soon offered to other customers.

Vehicles selected for rebuilding — Nationals and National 2s — were shipped to East Lancs (itself part of the Drawlane empire), where they were stripped and had new interior stress panels and external panelling fitted. Replacement window pans and doors were also installed, along with an extra entrance step. New front and rear ends were fitted, but the original chassis and ribbed roof were retained. The interior benefitted from DiPTAC fittings and new lighting. Mechanical work was carried out initially by London & Country but was later transferred to Blackburn Transport's workshops. A new engine — initially the Gardner 6HLXB (the Volvo THD100-series being a later option) — was fitted, and customers could also specify ZF or Voith transmission or retain the existing pneumocyclic system

Unsurprisingly, most of the rebuilds were for Drawlane companies, but among the customers from outside the group were Eastern Counties and the aforementioned Blackburn Transport, which latter had never previously operated Nationals of any kind. The biggest single customer, however, was London Buses, which had 42 of its National 2s rebuilt as Greenways for continued operation on Red Arrow services (along with an ex-Crosville bus for other work), and for which a revised frontal styling was developed. Altogether some 176 Greenways were produced.

Although the Greenway cost around half the price of a new bus it still represented a major investment and seemed even less of a bargain when compared price-wise to the lighter-weight Dennis Dart, which by now was taking the market by storm.

Northumbria Motor Services had been working on refurbishing Nationals and fitting a Cummins B-series engine before the operator became part of British Bus (as Drawlane had now become) in 1994. The project passed to London & Country, and thus was born the Urban Bus. The six-cylinder turbocharged engine was bought in, already mated to an Allison MT643 gearbox. A new radiator assembly and air intake were fitted, along with a replacement section of rear floor. Internally, the original seats were retained but refurbished, and the interior panels above the waistrail sprayed white. New interior lights were fitted. As on the Greenway, an extra entrance step was installed along with new doors. The dashboard was simplified. Externally the bus little was changed apart from new front and rear lights and engine access door. The engine air intake was moved to roof level.

Other operators also uprated their buses, among them Cheltenham & Gloucester, which introduced its own 'Leyland National 3', with DAF engine. A smart repaint and an upgraded interior, including new flooring, really did make a massive difference to the National experience.

GLS 443 (WLT 843) was rebuilt from National 2 (GUW 443W, and is seen here on Red Arrow route 507 bound for Waterloo in May 1994.
PRESBUS ARCHIVE

Midland Fox 2159 (JIL 2159) was rebuilt from Midland Red/Midland No 643 (PUK 643R). It is seen here in Leicester in 1995. PHILIP LAMB

Seen in January 1996 branded for Green Line route 415, PDZ 8273 had been rebuilt from Midland Red/Midland Fox 490 (JOX 490P) in October 1994. PHILIP LAMB

New to Southport and passing to Merseyside PTE, YFY 5M was rebuilt for Eastern Counties in May 1995 becoming LG785 in that fleet. PRESBUS ARCHIVE

New as West Yorkshire 3457 (GUA 821N) and rebuilt for London & Country in 1993, South Yorkshire 200 (NIW 6508) is pictured in its hometown of Pontefract. PRESBUS ARCHIVE

Starting out with East Kent, JJG 907P was reconstructed for Blackburn in 1994 becoming its 532. It is seen here at work in November 1996. PHILIP LAMB

Seen here in September 1997, PIJ 8104 was one of a pair of Volvo re-engined Nationals in the fleet of Paul S. Winson of Loughborough in the 1990s. One suspects that no B10M lurks beneath, and that the floor is no lower than it is in any other National — unless of course you know different . . .
PHILIP LAMB

Originally Maidstone & District 3548 (PKP 548R), Sussex Bus XIA 857 was one of two Urban Bus conversions used in the main on its Chichester–Petersfield service. Taken over by Stagecoach, XIA 857 was subsequently transferred to Devon. PHILIP LAMB

This National was new to Bristol Omnibus as C1461 (OAE 759R) in 1977. It was acquired by Volvo, and re-engined, served as a demonstrator. It is seen here on hire to Classic of Annfield Plain, which operator subsequently bought the bus. PRESBUS ARCHIVE

Advertising liveries

It would be a simple task to fill a whole magazine with advertising liveries, the Leyland National having been, over the years, the victim of many an 'over-the-top' scheme. Here are, with no comment as to taste, just three . . .

Liverbus 83 (PJI 5913) carries the message: 'Slow down, arrive late'. Previously registered RKA 874T, this National was new to Merseyside PTE, but had in the interim worked for Beestons of Hadleigh. PRESBUS ARCHIVE

Provincial 427 (BOU 4V) had been new to Bristol Omnibus in 1980 as its 3529. Seen here advertising Crown Bingo, it also spent a while extolling the benefits of the Bridge Centre in Portsmouth. PHILIP LAMB

In April 1988 the Meridian Conservatory Centre, Malden was making good use of Eastern National 1873 (ANO 272S). PRESBUS ARCHIVE

The End

All good things come to an end. In the case of many Leyland Nationals, certainly in the early days of the type's demise, they were put out to grass and stripped of spares to keep their brethren on the road, the resultant hulks being taken away to Barnsley in due course.

The end had well and truly arrived for these Halton Nationals seen at the back of the operator's Moor Lane garage in 1999. Awaiting disposal, having been cannibalised for spares, are, nearest the camera first: 22 (BTB 22T) (bought new 1979), 21 (ACW 921R) (bought new 1977), 2 (MDL 880R) (ex-Southern Vectis 1987) 24 (BTB 24T) (bought new 1979) and 19 (ACW 219R) (bought new 1977).

A visit to Midland Red West's Worcester garage in May 1998 revealed this pair of Leyland Nationals awaiting their fate. They are Nos 749/58 (XOV 749/58T). Pictures: PHILIP LAMB

Nationals in preservation

Many Leyland Nationals have found their way into preservation. Here are just a few caught on camera in the last few years.

Midland Red West 544 (NOE 544R) is in preservation at the Transport Museum, Wythall, where a large collection of buses which operated in the Midlands over several decades is housed. **Pictures:** PHILIP LAMB

Seen at a running day in Kirkby, Liverpool is Merseyside Transport 1000 (OHF 858S), one of a number of buses in preservation with John Cherry of Bootle.

Leaving Salisbury bus station in January 2014 we see Hants & Dorset 3645 (GLJ 681N) in preservation with a Mr Johnson. The occasion was the last day of operation at the bus station.

Another Leyland National preserved at the Transport Museum, Wythall is National 2 West Midlands 1026 (DOC 36V).

Last of a long line! National 2 Halton 33 (C49 OCM) was the very last Leyland National to roll off the production line.

One of the most popular marques with one of the most popular operators — Paul Llewellyn's Southdown 34 (PCD 80R) pauses outside Worthing railway station.

New to South Yorkshire PTE as its 1076, National 2 FWA 475V is preserved in the colours of later owner Isle Coaches of Owston Ferry.

Seen elsewhere in this publication when in service with East Midland/ Mansfield & District, Hastings & District VKE 566S takes a turn on the free service at the South East Vehicle Show at the Kent Showground in 2013.

National 2 Lancashire Travel 6156 (XLV 156W) was new to Merseyside PTE and is today preserved by Messers Johnson and Hillan of St Helens.

London Country LNB312 (UPB 312S), seen here in Hemel Hempstead, is preserved in original guise by Messers Berg and Bedford of New Haw, Surrey.

National 2 Yorkshire Traction 245 (NKU 245X) is preserved in West Yorkshire Metro livery by Keighley Bus Museum member Mick Jessop.

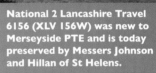

The National in preservation

With the help of some of the best-known Leyland National preservationists we look at the type in preservation.

Leyland Nationals London Country SNB312 (UPB 312S) and Alder Valley 127 (KCG 627L) meet at Great Missenden railway station whilst taking past in the 2007 Amersham Running Day. MICK BERG

Today Leyland Nationals no longer clatter in bus stations across the country or can even be found carting astonished schoolchildren in rural backwaters, so it's left to preservationists to spread the word, sounds and exhaust smoke.

The last major operator, Chase Coaches of Chase Terrace, Staffordshire went down with its Nationals when it was taken over by Arriva in April 2007. Chase had maintained its Nationals superbly and by modifying air intakes managed to get the best out of 30-year-old examples. It was ironic that for the first few weeks of operating former Chase services Arriva found itself forced to use some of the inherited Nationals, even treating (?) a couple to aquamarine and stone fronts and its own branding. The buses were all sold off at an auction held at the former Chase premises on 19 May 1997.

Today Go-Ahead-owned Konectbus in Norfolk has a National used on special duties, but nowhere is there a substantial fleet of Nationals. Preservationists seemed to have been late to cotton on to the National, maybe because of its ubiquity and the struggle to save other types. One former Southdown example has been at the Science Museum, Wroughton, since the 1980s, but it is generally acknowledged that the first National to be preserved privately, ex-London Country HPF 318N, was purchased by Michael Trew as late as 1991. Experts reckon that today there are around 100 Nationals in active preservation and as many again in various states of restoration.

Many of the buses that had been hanging around awaiting a saviour have now been scrapped, and operators have dispensed with spares. A few specialists, notably Mike Nash of British Bus Sales, who has gone out of his way to save rare National variants, and Mark Owen of

Central Bus Restorations, will help where they can, but they don't have unlimited stocks. Before we go through what to look for on a National, let's first speak to some of the preservationists and specialists most associated with the type.

Mike Lloyd — National maintainer

Mike, who worked for London Country as a fitter at Hemel Hempstead from 1977 to 1981 and was foreman at St Albans for the next three years, had dozens of Nationals to look after. 'I have several preserved vehicles of my own, but I really admire anyone who successfully preserves Nationals. They were terrible in service. Our Merlins were more reliable.' But, despite his apparently dim view of the type, Mike is full of admiration for the National's body structure. 'It was as tough as old boots, and you certainly wouldn't want to argue with one of these buses in any other vehicle.'

Mike's scepticism over the National's reliability arises from a feeling that mechanical units were built down to a price rather than up to a specification. 'Everything was air-operated. The air-compressor was quite small. They used to pump oil into the air system. The wiring loom came into section; they used something called a military connector. They screwed together and were supposed to be weatherproof, though they weren't. On the original National the voltage-control unit was mounted inside the bumper under the filler to the radiator, so every day they were treated to a good dose of cold water. I think they thought if there was a space they should bung something it.'

There was always trouble with the airbags and suspension on the Nationals. 'They were mounted on pedestals made of aluminium, which reacts with steel. The control rods for the suspension-levelling bags could corrode and the compressor, so vitally needed with all the air to provide, was water-cooled on the head and the rest air cooled.' He adds: 'Brake balance was wrong on early buses — the rear brakes could only last a fortnight in service, and the front brakes could practically seize up through lack of use.' On the credit side, a National 510 engine could, to its maintainers' surprise, run without water. 'We had drained the water out of a bus, and while we went to get the antifreeze the driver took it away and used it on a complete duty. When the bus got back we filled it with water and changed the oil, and we had at least a further two years out of that engine.' Finally, Mike pays testimony to the National's strength. 'Early one morning an inexperienced driver lost control of a National two

Seen in service on the contents page in later Halton livery, Widnes No 1 (RTC 645L) was the first single-door municipal National, and is today preserved ay the North West Museum of Road Transport. PHILIP LAMB

miles out of Hemel. It turned the bus into a half-cab. When they towed it in there was blood in the cab. The driver had cut his hand. That was all that was wrong with him.'

Eddie Knorn — preservationist and member of the Leyland National Group

Eddie has 'lost count' of the Nationals he's owned and shares in over the years, buying his first example, former London Country UPB 312S, from Cowie in 1997. 'It was relatively unmolested and didn't need too much doing to it,' he recalls. A current major project is UPE 203M, latterly with St John Ambulance.
'It all depends what you are looking for — whether you want an original National or a converted bus. But don't forget that just about any bus will have had some conversion work done to it. Normally the electrics can be coped with, though they were installed in modules and there can be some strange connections between them.'
Adds Eddie: 'Keep on top of any little breakages; for example the fuel pump can play up a bit.' He also recommends regular oil changes for the 510 engine. 'Bodily, window pans can crumble away, meaning water attacks the main pillars.'
He advises that vehicles be

kept under cover and that it's worth checking the past of a potential purchase. 'Buses from operators such as Northumbria have been through a lot of bad weather and salt on the road,' he warns.
The Leyland National Group (HYPERLINK "http://www.leylandnationgroup.co.uk" www.leylandnationgroup.co.uk) was formed in 1997 and aims to help National owners in any way possible. 'A lot of preservationists who have Nationals know each other, and there's a good support network,' says Eddie.

Mike Nash — dealer/collector/National fanatic

Mike bought his first National in 1997 and has since collected, sold and resold dozens of examples. He offers sensible advice to National buyers. 'Go for the best one you can find — unless you really want a vehicle from a particular dealer or operator. They are expensive things to put right nowadays. You can't buy engines like you used to, and no-one wants to fix 510s.' He adds that a lot of the one-time best buses around have fallen by the roadside. 'It's wise to go for a bus with little visible rust as possible. 'We can't get hold of window pans now, for example.'
Earlier vehicles seem to have better build quality and

superior corrosion resistance, according to Mike. He adds that operators often simplified electrical circuits on the buses, but advises that these be checked over by an electrical expert. 'Make sure batteries have some charge in them; otherwise the alternator, regulator and their connections can suffer if you try to jump-start them. They are very sensitive in this respect.' The notorious

Leyland 510 engine he has never found to be a problem. 'We've never known one to go bang, but they do need oil changes.'

Mark Owen — proprietor of Central Bus Restorations and owner of three Nationals

Mark's father used to drive National 2s for Midland Red, and he has two Midland Red National 2s (BVP 808/11V) and National (NOE 600R). 'I seem to have specialised in Nationals to some degree and am able to inspect them for would-be customers,' he says, adding: 'Condition of the stress panels is important. Chassis can fracture at the back end, particularly when a more powerful engine, such as the Volvo, has been fitted.' Mark also feels that the 510 engine was relatively reliable, although pipework should be inspected; 'Don't forget that a lot of these vehicles will have been thrashed by drivers at some time.'

What to look for when buying a National

So, it seems from the experts we've spoken to that a National can be a good preservation prospect, although they are no longer around in the numbers they once were. The bodywork is extremely strong (although corrosion can take hold), the 510 engine isn't a terror in preservation if you change the oil regularly and generally look after it, but you need to have someone who knows something about electrics.